Forgive the River, Forgive the Sky

Forgive the River, Forgive the Sky

Gloria Whelan

Eerdmans Books for Young Readers
Grand Rapids, Michigan

Copyright © 1998 by Gloria Whelan
Published 1998 by Eerdmans Books for Young Readers
an imprint of Wm. B. Eerdmans Publishing Co.
255 Jefferson Ave. S.E., Grand Rapids, Michigan 49503 /
P.O. Box 163, Cambridge CB3 9PU U.K.

Paperback edition 1999

Printed in the United States of America

07 06 05 04 03   8 7 6 5 4 3

Library of Congress Cataloging-in-Publication Data

Whelan, Gloria.
Forgive the river, forgive the sky / by Gloria Whelan.
p.   cm.
Summary: After her father dies in the river they both love, twelve-year-old Lily struggles to
come to terms with her loss,
and in so doing, she helps a paraplegic former pilot accept
his condition and move on with his life.
ISBN 0-8028-5256-4 (pbk. : alk. paper)
[1. Grief—Fiction.   2. River life—Michigan—Fiction.
3. Physically handicapped—Fiction.   4. Michigan—Fiction.]
I. Title.
PZ7.W5718Fo   1998
[Fic]—dc21   97-14257
CIP
AC
www.eerdmans.com

In memory of my father,
William Rewoldt,
who taught me to love the river

ONE

From halfway up the oak tree I watched the fence go up. The first section of the fence shut off the place where last year I found four different colors of violets growing all at once: white, yellow, lavender, and purple. It was our land the men were fencing off. Only we didn't own it anymore. Someone named T. R. Tracy owned it. I told myself it still belonged to us. Like the time I spent weeks squeezing together a thousand tiny links to make a bracelet for my best friend, Laura. I know it's hers because I gave it to her, but she'll never know it like I do.

The land that Mom sold had forty acres of woods and a little pond. That's not all that unusual in this part of northern Michigan. Woods is about all there is.

What made our land so valuable is the Sandy River. The Sandy is just about the finest trout river in the world. The cabin where I grew up sits right on a bend of the river. Mr. Tracy lives in the cabin now.

When Dad died last year, Mom said we'd have to sell our land and move into town. I said I wouldn't go. I'd run away and live in the woods and they'd never find me. I'd eat berries and roots until I starved. I said all that would be left of me was a bunch of white bones like the ones I once found next to a fox's hole. Of course I gave in and moved to town with Mom. I told myself it would serve the river right if I deserted it. The thing is, angry as I am at the river because of what happened to my dad, I can't stay away from it.

The link fence the men were putting up was heavy duty. To cut it, which I planned to do, I'd have to snitch a good wire cutter. It wouldn't really be snitching because we own a hardware store. Star Hardware. It's been in the family for three generations. Someday I'll run it. I borrow a lot of stuff from our tool rental. Hidden beside the oak tree I was sitting in was a bag with a crowbar and a claw hammer. I sneaked them out of the store for something I planned to do on my way home.

I waited until the men putting up the fence had moved on, and then I climbed down from the tree, tearing my jeans. Somewhere in the tree was the band that holds my hair back so it doesn't look like a frizzled cloud. There was a button off my shirt, too. Neatness is not my thing. I once heard a boy in school say I looked like I had been pulled through a hedge. My mother actually bought me a dress and insisted I put it on for church, but it showed my scabby knees and all the briar scratches on my legs, so I didn't have to wear it after all.

Picking up my bag with the tools, I headed back toward town. In the woods the early flowers, spring beauties and Dutchman's-breeches and trout lilies, had all disappeared. The only things in bloom were the trillium and a few starflowers, like my name, Lily Star.

I wove a wreath with the starflowers and the trillium. Kneeling beside the river, I laid the wreath on the water and watched the quick current snatch it and carry it away. In the year since my father died, I had made a wreath every week to send down the river. In the fall I used orange and red leaves and the spidery

3

gold flowers of witch hazel; in the winter I wove the wreaths from pine and hemlock branches. When the snow cleared, I made my wreaths from pussy willows and moss. I knew every inch of the river and the speed of the current. I knew exactly when the wreath would be carried over the spot where my father died.

There were people who said my father had a happy death. He died of a heart attack fishing in the river he loved. But he was wading the river late at night when a hatch was on. So he died all alone in the dark. I see it happening in my nightmares. Over and over. Much as I love the river, I can't forgive it.

Everything changed after Dad's death. Dad had spent more time fishing than he had in our hardware store. I'd get up early in the morning and find him and his trout rod gone. I'd run down to the river and there he'd be. "Bring me a hot cup of coffee, Lily," he'd call, "and you can try a few casts. The trout are plenty hungry this morning." If the trout kept biting, Dad wouldn't get to the store until afternoon.

After he died, Mom spent a lot of nights shuffling papers and huddling with Betty Merker, the manager of our bank. Mom found out that Dad had taken out loans on the store. I guess he spent too much time fishing and not enough time working. That left Mom with all these debts. She was plenty unhappy, but she just gritted her teeth. She's got this independent thing. She doesn't want to owe anyone anything. After we sold our property to pay the loans, we moved into a little apartment above the hardware store, and Mom took over the business. She doesn't like working there. She liked it when she worked at May's Country Cupboard, a gift store, where she was selling pretty things. Now she has to sell bolts and nails and wrestle fifty-pound bags of fertilizer. She hates all that stuff because it smells bad and breaks her nails.

I like the hardware store, but I hate living over it. Instead of seeing woods when I look out of my window, I see Pete's Bar and Grill sign flicking off and on like some gaudy stars. Instead of hearing the river, I hear cars rushing up the expressway from downstate and then rushing back again.

ૐ   ૐ   ૐ

On the way to town I stopped at the Bad Hads' shack. That's Hadden and Hadley Durwood. They're twins that live together. Neither one of them is married, which doesn't surprise me. No women could stand to get within a hundred feet of their shack. They throw everything out their back door, including their garbage. I could see tin cans lying in the tall grass like rusty flowers. Their beagle was sitting on top of an old crate, barking like crazy.

I skulked around in the trees. When I was sure the Bad Hads weren't there, I unchained their dog, Fleabit. He's skinny and full of fleas. He didn't even have a name until I gave him one. The twins just called him "Dog."

Fleabit was all over me, trying to get to the dog biscuits in my pocket. When he had eaten them, he chased his tail for a while and rolled around on the grass to scratch his fleas. Then I had to chain him up again. A couple of times a week I bring Fleabit something to eat and unhitch him. I have to be sure the Bad Hads are out doing errands or hunting, which is often. They kill anything that swims, has wings, or moves on four legs. In season or out. Mostly out.

Leaving the shack, I followed the river for a mile until I came to a pine tree on which a small platform had been built. Across the river was a taller pine. On top of that taller tree was a ragged nest made up of messy tangles of sticks. A great black bird with a white head and tail and a hooked yellow beak was hunkered down on the nest. The bird, a bald eagle, spread its great wings and flew off. It soared until it was a black dot in the blue sky.

I looked around to be sure I was alone. Slinging the bag holding the hammer and crowbar over my shoulder, I climbed the strips of wood someone had nailed to the tree to make steps up to the platform. After I pried up a lot of the platform's planks, I climbed down the ladder, knocking loose each rung above me until the ladder disappeared. I was anxious to finish so the eagle could return to its nest.

The Rivertown *Avalanche* had run an article about some scientists. They planned to come up from the university on weekends to observe the eagles' nest. They were going to drag floodlights and camera equipment up to the platform. I worried that all the commotion would make the eagles fly away. Eagles are really solitary and secretive. I like that. I wanted the eagle to stay on its nest.

It was late afternoon when I got back to town. Rivertown leans against woods on one side. The Sandy River has its arm around it on the other side. All there is to the town is Ben's Pizza Shop, the Rivertown bank, the supermarket, Pete's Bar and Grill, May's Country Cupboard, Value Drugs, our church, and Star Hardware. We also have fake Christmas wreaths with big red plastic bows on all the light poles. They're put up by the Rivertown Chamber of Commerce. Even though it was June, no one had bothered to take them down. They get around leaving the decorations up by having a Christmas-in-September sale at all the stores.

I was sneaking in the hardware store to put back the claw hammer and crowbar. Charlie, who works in the store, caught me. He's pretty old, with a gray beard and pale, watery, red eyes that look like holes in his head. You can always tell what he's had to eat from the crumbs in his beard. This time it looked like chocolate doughnuts. Charlie lives alone, so Mom has him over for dinner on days like Thanksgiving and Christmas and anytime she makes chili, which is his favorite.

"So that's where the crowbar went," Charlie said.

"Someone was here after one, and I looked high and low for it. I'd like to see what all you do with our tools, Lily." He ran his fingers through his beard, and I watched some of the crumbs fly off. "On the other hand, maybe I wouldn't."

I told him about the scientists and the eagle.

"Well, Lily, you're only twelve, so you wouldn't remember, but ten years ago we didn't have any eagles around here. Those scientists you don't like are the ones who found out that DDT was having a bad effect on eagle eggs. When DDT was banned, we had eagles again. How about after work I give you a ride out to the tree, and you and I put the platform and the steps back?"

I didn't say no.

"Right now your Ma is looking for you. Now that school is out, you could give her a hand around here. When I was twelve like you, I was working eight hours a day cutting trees."

I wondered if he had had his beard when he was twelve. I couldn't imagine him without it.

In the front of the store, the Bad Hads were buying a length of chain from Mom. They were trying to talk down the price, something they always do. You can tell them apart because Hadden wears his baseball cap with the bill to the front, and Hadley wears his with the bill to the back. No one's ever seen them without their caps. They're both as tall and thin as saplings. "Mean 'n lean" is the way Dad described them. They never look right at you, only sidewise like birds do.

Hadden was lecturing Mom. "You should never have sold your property, Irene. The man that bought it is puttin' a fence around it. We've been huntin' that land for thirty years. And our dad before us. Now what? Who does he think he is? No one's seen him. Why's that? He must be hidin' something. I wouldn't be surprised if he was runnin' away from the law."

I couldn't keep my mouth shut. "You mean the law might be after him because he's been poaching deer?"

The Hads gave me a dirty look, since they poach all the time. It used to drive Dad crazy, especially when they did it on our land.

Hadley said, "Look who's talkin'. I seen you over near our place. That's trespassin', and that's against the law." He turned to Mom. "You keep your girl away from our place, Irene."

Mom doesn't like the Bad Hads any more than I do. Her voice was icy cold. "I'm sure Lily would find nothing to interest her at your place." Mom reminds me of a chipmunk. She's small, with brown eyes and short, shiny brown hair, and she's pert and lively. The Hads could look sidewise at her all they wanted and she wouldn't care.

After they left, Mom set me to straightening the shelves and putting out the new merchandise. There isn't enough money to buy a lot of stock, so there's mostly only one or two of everything. I put stuff right at the edge of the shelf so it looks like there's more than there is. After work, Charlie and I went to the pine tree across from the eagle's nest. We hammered the platform back together and replaced the steps. So it wasn't until after supper that I got to take my canoe out. Since Mom and I moved from the river, Mr. Borcher lets me keep it at his canoe livery in town.

I let the current carry me downriver. I was doing a little fishing, casting out the line and then holding it still for a minute on the backstroke to let it straighten out. It was the way my dad had showed me. I tried to snap it into the little riffles at the edges of the moss-covered logs that hugged the shore. Red-winged black-birds were jumping up and down on the alder bushes, spreading their wings to show off their shoulder patches. Their shrieky calls said, "This is my space. You get away."

I knew how they felt. It was how I felt about some-one else living on our land. I guided the canoe toward what used to be our cabin. There's a landing dock in front of the cabin with a bench on it. Dad and I used to sit there looking up and down the bend. If you stay really quiet, you can spot otters sliding down the bank, or blue herons high-stepping along the river, spearing frogs with their long beaks.

I felt awful looking from the outside at the place where I used to be inside. Our old cabin seemed deserted. I was just thinking about beaching the canoe and looking in the windows when a light went on. I decided I had better get out of there. There was some-thing mysterious about T. R. Tracy. Even Mom had never met him. When the sale was made, a lawyer signed all the papers for him. Mom had talked to Mr. Tracy on the phone. She had offered to show him around the house, tell him where the septic tank was, and explain what to do when the front door stuck. He had said thanks but no thanks. He didn't even do his grocery shopping in Rivertown. People saw his van headed in the direction of the next town.

I turned the canoe around and started back up the river. For a mile or two I really hated T. R. Tracy, who was living in our cabin and fencing me out of our land. But a mink started playing tag with the canoe, swimming around it and diving under one side and coming up on the other side. So I forgot about Mr. Tracy. You really have to concentrate to hate someone.

TWO

I hung around the store most of the next day. It was Friday, the beginning of the weekend. People from downstate would be coming up to fish the Sandy River. Dad had always told them what kind of fishing tackle to buy. He had kept a supply of artificial flies, too, and could tell which one to use depending on what insects were flying around the river. Mom doesn't know anything about that stuff. She depends on me because I used to fish with Dad all the time. Sometimes we'd fish from the canoe; sometimes we'd wade the river. Right now I was saving for some new waders.

When some preppy with neatly pressed khaki pants and a funny hat stuck all over with artificial flies comes in, he isn't exactly happy about a twelve-year-old giving him advice. After we talk a while, though, he stops treating me like some smart-mouthed brat and starts paying attention.

Around two I went out for a Coke with Laura Schawn, who is my best friend. We'll be in seventh grade next year. Laura and I don't look at all alike. She's got this perfect, sleek blonde hair that looks like she's always combing it, which she isn't because she's not like that. I'm tall and gangling with washed-out brown hair that frizzes up into a bird's nest if there's even one drop of rain in the air. Laura is a little spacey and forgets things like when she's supposed to meet you. But you can't get mad at her because she has this friendly face. It's round with big round eyes. She looks like the kind of person you make when you first learn to draw. Unlike me, she's an indoor person who is always doing crafts. Their house is full of stuff made of pinecones and shells and dried flowers. Sometimes I think a hot glue gun is actually part of Laura's arm. But she's really loyal to her friends.

Once in my sixth grade class everyone had to give a report on how to identify mammals. I brought the droppings I collected in the woods from raccoons, porcupines, and deer to show the differences. Even though I had put everything in neat plastic bags, the teacher wanted to throw the droppings and me with them out of the room.

Laura raised her hand and said that I had showed her a book a real scientist had written about that stuff and that it was a scientific way to recognize an animal. Later she told me what I did was the grossest thing she had ever seen.

Laura's dad is an assessor for the township. He checks out houses to see how much they're worth so he can figure out what the taxes are going to be. I could see she had some news she was dying to tell me. "Dad went to the Tracy place," she said.

"I wish you wouldn't call it that." I still thought of the land as ours. "Was Mr. Tracy there?"

"No. Dad just looked through the windows."

I asked, "What's it like inside?" But I wasn't sure I wanted to know. I wanted to keep thinking of it just the way it was when we lived there.

"There were a lot of airplane models hanging from the ceiling. Otherwise it was mostly empty except for some chairs and tables and a bed. He said the cabin didn't look lived in. I think it's a hideout."

Laura has a super imagination. "From what?"

"Maybe Mr. Tracy escaped from jail or some foreign country."

I thought she might be right. If he didn't have something to hide, why would he want to put a fence around himself?

❧   ❧   ❧

A few days later, T. R. Tracy did something even more stupid than putting up a fence. Mom had given me the afternoon off so I could go fishing.

Fishing is my way of feeling close to my dad. He and I had been out on the river in every season and all kinds of weather. Every April he let me skip school on the day that trout season opened. Sometimes it was so cold we had to beach the canoe and build a fire to warm our fingers so we could keep casting. We were out all summer, too, even on a rainy day when you had a hard time telling whether the dimples in the water were raindrops or trout rising. In the fall the summer fishermen were gone, and we fished with the bright colors of the leaves and the smell of wood smoke from the cabins along the river. It was always a sad time because we knew winter was coming and there would be an end to our days on the river.

Sometimes I go over Dad's fishing diary. He kept it from the time he was a boy. It shows when and where he fished—near the swamp, on the high banks, or just below the bridge. It tells what flies he used, maybe a coachman or a streamer, and what the weather was like. There might have been a hatch on or a light rain. It even lists the number and size of the trout. A lot of the time there's a note saying, "Lily was with me."

I was drifting along the river, thinking of all those times Dad and I had fished. The afternoon sun lit up the water so I could see the ripples of sand and the bright stones on the river bottom. As the boat rounded the bend, I noticed one of the men who had been putting up the fence. I didn't recognize him, so he wasn't a local. He must have been from some downstate construction company. He was pounding a row of cedar logs into the river bottom. The logs were like a stockade shutting off T. R. Tracy's landing.

"What do you think you're doing?" I screeched at him.

He looked at me like I was something that had crawled up from the river bottom. "What I'm paid to do. Give the guy a little privacy."

"If you leave those stakes in, they'll change the course of the river. Anyhow, they look terrible."

"That's none of my business. And I'd guess it's none of yours." He began pounding again.

I turned my canoe around and headed upriver toward town. There was no way I was going to let those logs stay there. I felt like a vampire must feel when some busybody drives a stake through its heart. It's true I was angry with the river, but I still couldn't let anything bad happen to it.

❧   ❧   ❧

Two nights later I was back with a rubber mallet in my canoe. You have to understand about the river at night. It's not just a straight shot downstream. There are sandbars where you can get stuck and stumps in the middle of the river below water level that can knock a hole in your boat. There are sharp bends where the current takes you where you don't want to go. Worst of all are the sweepers, dead trees that lean out over the river. If you don't see them, they can sweep you into the water.

Even though I know every inch of the river, Mom doesn't like me to take the canoe out alone at night. But I knew she would never find out because it was Midnight Madness in Rivertown. The Chamber of Commerce had planned a night when all the stores were open until midnight and had big sales going on. Mom said it was too late for me to be up, so she got Ben Baker to help her. He's a deputy sheriff and has eight kids, so he always needs extra money. Mom was at the store thinking I was safe in bed. I eased the canoe into the river and headed for Mr. Tracy's. In spite of a bright moon, it was hard to see. The day had been steamy hot, but the river never stands still, so it's always cold. That meant there was a fog over the river. Dad called it "a dance of veils."

An animal was moving along the shore, maybe a raccoon after crayfish or a fox nosing around for ducklings. There was a caddis hatch on, and clouds of fish flies were sneaking out of the water to try their wings. A bat was swinging through the air like a trapeze artist, gulping down the flies.

Because of the fog, it took me extra long to reach the cabin. I was relieved to see everything was dark. The river was shallow at the landing, only up to my knees. I tied my boat up to a tree and waded into the freezing river. I started to pry one of the logs free, giving it some swings with the mallet. Because the mallet was rubber, it hardly made any noise. After a few whacks the log loosened. I yanked it free and gave it a push down the river. One after another I loosened the logs. It took nearly an hour. As the last one floated away, I heard a noise. When I looked up, I saw a light go on and a door open. A flashlight swept over me. A second later I had the canoe untied and was paddling upriver as fast as I could. I started worrying about what I had done. I remembered the warning my dad used to give me: "Don't just do something, Lily, stand there."

I made it home and under the covers only minutes before Mom got there. I called out to let her know I was awake. She came into my bedroom, flung herself into a chair, and stretched out her legs. "As far as I'm concerned, the next time the Chamber of Commerce thinks up something like this, they can stay up all night themselves and do the selling. I broke another nail, and right in the middle of the rush Ben got a call from Sheriff Bronson and had to take off. The sheriff wanted Ben to go out on a call. Evidently something was going on at our old place. I can't imagine what it was."

"Who called the sheriff?"

"The mysterious Mr. Tracy."

"Did Ben say what was wrong?" My heart was pounding so hard I wondered if Mom could see my chest bumping the covers up and down.

"Some sort of vandalism. We certainly never had anything like that when we lived there."

"He shouldn't have put a fence up."

"No. I'm sure that made him enemies. Still, that doesn't excuse breaking the law. After all, it's his land to do with as he pleases. Now you better go back to sleep. Pleasant dreams, sweetie."

My dreams weren't pleasant. I dreamed I was in prison and the Bad Hads were the jailers and wouldn't give me anything to eat but dog biscuits.

THREE

It was halfway through June, and I wanted to see the moccasin flowers on our land before they were done blooming. They're my favorite. So I borrowed a wire cutter from the store and took off. The last of the fence was up, and there was a lock on the gate. That meant that I could never walk over the land that I had grown up on, land that Dad and I had walked over hundreds of times. I picked a section of the fence hidden behind a thicket of blackberry briars and tried to cut a hole in it. I wasn't getting very far. I didn't have the strength to cut through the heavy wire. I was squeezing away and sort of grunting when I heard a whirring sound. It was like the noise a ruffed grouse makes when it flies up. Suddenly there was this man in an electric wheelchair making for me a mile a minute. I was so startled I couldn't even run.

"Just what do you think you're doing?"

I looked through the fence at the man's angry face and froze. The problem I have is that I can't lie. Whenever anyone asks me something, even if I don't mean to, I tell the truth. "I was trying to cut a hole in your fence."

"I can see that. What I want to know is why." He was plenty mad.

"So I can crawl through."

"If I find you anywhere near my property again, inside or outside the fence, I'll call the sheriff on you." Suddenly he looked more closely at me. "I recognize you. You're the girl who knocked down my stakes. I've got a good notion to have you locked up. I didn't move two hundred miles from the city to have juvenile delinquents swarming over my land."

By now I was getting as angry as he was. "I'm not a juvenile delinquent."

"Just who are you, then?"

"My dad and his family owned this land for a long time before you did. My greatgrandfather lived here when he worked for a logging camp."

"You must be Irene Star's girl. I bought this land from your mother, and I paid a good price for it. You don't have any business here."

He had sort of calmed down, so I wasn't afraid to look at him. He was about my dad's age. If he had been standing instead of sitting in a wheelchair, he would have been tall. He was fishbelly pale with short black hair and eyes the color of a blue jay. He had a sort of dazed look, like he'd walked from a dark room into the sunlight.

"This property has never been fenced," I said. "Why do you want to shut people out?"

"I'm not shutting people out. I'm shutting myself in. Now do me a favor and clear out."

❧   ❧   ❧

I slunk away, but the next day I was back with my dad's binoculars and a new notebook that cost me seventy-five cents. I was going to write down every suspicious thing I saw. I hid behind a couple of pine trees, where I could keep an eye on the cabin. I'd decided the Bad Hads and Laura were probably right. T. R. Tracy was some kind of dangerous character hiding out from the law.

Sure enough. The door to the cabin opened, and the man wheeled himself out. He had binoculars that he trained on the sky. About half an hour from Rivertown there's this training base for the National Guard. Their planes fly over the town all the time. I watched T. R. Tracy through *my* binoculars watching the planes through *his* binoculars. He was making notes. I made notes about his making notes. Maybe he was going to sell information about the planes to our enemies, whoever they were. I don't keep up with that international stuff where everyone's shooting at everyone else.

Just then a pileated woodpecker landed on the pine tree next to me and started hammering away like crazy. T. R. Tracy swung around, and the next thing I knew we were looking at each other through our binoculars. He wheeled over to the fence. I should have run, but I just stood there with my mouth open.

"You might as well come out. I can see you. What do you think you're doing? Just why are you spying on me?"

"Why are you spying on the planes?"

"I'm not spying. I happen to be interested in planes."

I remembered how Laura had said there were lots of model planes in the cabin. He looked at the expression on my face and laughed. "O.K., Mata Hari," he said. I guess Mata Hari was some kind of famous spy lady. "I'll show you what I'm talking about." He unlocked the gate and motioned me to follow him into the cabin.

I was a little scared, but curiosity got the best of me. The cabin was just the way Laura described it—empty except for what he needed just to live. There were planes, large ones and small ones, scattered around the room and hanging from the ceiling. "Aren't you a little old for model planes?" I asked.

"These aren't the kind of planes you buy in a kit. I make them from scratch, and they're one of a kind."

"What do you mean?"

"Well, look at the shape of this one's wings."

The plane had a kind of kink in its wings that made it look like an osprey when it flies. I could see the planes were carefully made. They weren't just crafts like Laura does. They were more like something you'd see in a museum if there were museums for model planes. "You're not a spy or a criminal or anything?"

"Of course not. Whatever gave you that idea?"

"Well, it looked like you were hiding out."

"I just don't want to get involved with people." His voice got a little angry. "What's the matter with my wanting a little privacy?"

"Well, there are things I ought to be keeping track of here. Since you put your fence up, I can't."

"You mean you want to keep track of something besides me?"

"A lot of things. I don't even know if the beavers still have their lodge in the pond or if the loon is back on its nest."

He gave me a long look, like he was re-reading something in a book he didn't understand the first time around. "I guess losing your father and then this land was hard. I've had a little bad luck myself. I'll tell you what. Since you used to live here, you can have a key to the lock on the gate, but you're not to give it to anyone else."

When he handed me the key, I was too startled even to thank him. He grinned at me and said, "I'll tell you something. I waited until you had a chance to get away the other night before I called the sheriff." He turned on the motor of his wheelchair and whizzed away, leaving me with my mouth open

❧   ❧   ❧

I didn't want to push my luck by tramping over his land right away, so I waited a whole day. I couldn't wait any longer than that because I knew the moccasin flowers would be gone. I didn't want to miss them.

As I walked down the driveway, Mr. Tracy wheeled down the path to meet me. "You want to see some flowers?" I asked.

"No. I couldn't care less about flowers."

"If you don't care about what's on your land, why did you come here?"

"Because it's nowhere."

I wondered what the Rivertown Chamber of Commerce would think about that. "Have you always been in a wheelchair?"

"No."

"Why are you in one now?"

"Because I can't use my legs."

"What kind of work did you do before the accident?"

"You ask too many questions." With that he whirred away.

The moccasin flowers were on the riverbank about a quarter of a mile from the house. The blossoms are a rosy pink and all puffed up, with hundreds of tiny veins crisscrossing them like little roads. Some people call them lady slippers, but I call them moccasin flowers. I like to think of Indians along the river. A long time ago the Indians used rivers like expressways to travel across the state on their way from Lake Huron to Lake Michigan. The Indians kept to the river, and the river fed them: crayfish, grayling, trout, duck, and beaver. I've even found arrowheads in the sand. Dad used to say the reason the river chatters so much is that it has so many stories to tell.

I had my shoes off and was wading in the river. I could feel the swift current sweeping the sand from under my feet in a way that tickled. As I reached for some watercress to chew for its peppery taste, I saw a bright red gleam on the riverbank. At first I thought it might be some sort of flower, but when I got closer I discovered it was a scarlet tanager. You see scarlet tanagers flashing through the trees like little flames. I had never seen one close up. It was bright red all over except for its black wings. All huddled down in the grass it looked dead, but when I picked it up, it fluttered in my hand. I was so startled I nearly dropped it.

I could see right away what was wrong. It had a fish hook with an artificial fly stuck right through its beak. The fish hook was attached to the fine thread of a leader. Someone must have been casting for trout, and the tanager saw the fly in the air and not the fishline. When the bird snatched at the fly, the hook caught it. The fisherman must have panicked and cut his line. With the hook in its bill, the bird was starving to death.

I stuck my wet feet into my shoes and took off with the bird cradled in my hands. Five minutes later I was running up a ramp and pounding on T. R. Tracy's door. He opened the door with an angry look. "What do you want now? What are you doing with that dead bird?"

"It's not dead. Honest."

I think he was ready to slam the door in my face. "When I gave you permission to come here, I didn't expect you to make a nuisance of yourself."

"The bird isn't dead. But if you keep shouting at me, it'll die of fright. It's got a hook in its mouth. We've got to get the hook out and give it some food. It's starving."

I guess Mr. Tracy finally realized how upset I was. He calmed down and looked more closely at the bird. "I've never seen a bird like that. What do you call it?"

"It's a scarlet tanager. Are you going to do something?"

He sighed. "All right. Just this once. Let me get a clippers." He whirred away and was back in a minute. Gently he took the bird from me and snipped off the hook's barb, then drew the hook out of the bird's beak. The bird rested in his hand, making only a few fluttering movements. "It might be better just to let the bird die," he said. There was a sort of sad, faraway look on his face. He turned to me. "Now what?"

"You need to mix egg with a little pabulum and give it to the bird with an eye dropper."

His eyebrows went up. "How do you know that?"

"My dad raised some birds once from a nest in a tree that had been cut down."

"Fine. You take it home and do that." Mr. Tracy

started to push me toward the door.

"I can't."

"What do you mean you can't?"

"You have to feed the bird every hour or so, and Mom works at the hardware store, and so do I a lot of the time. But I've got my bike. I could go to the store and get the pabulum. I could pay for it, Mr. Tracy."

Mr. Tracy gave me a twisty smile, with one corner of his mouth turned down and the other up. It looked as though only half of him wanted to smile. "You win," he said. He reached into his pocket and handed me some money. "If the bird is to be a guest in my house, I'll be responsible for its keep. And call me T. R."

❧   ❧   ❧

That afternoon I told Mom about T. R. and how he was taking care of the bird, and wouldn't you know she thought I was "imposing." She thinks things have to be completely equal between people. What I mean is she keeps score. If someone does something for you, you have to do something back right away. You can't wait. I just figure eventually it will all even out.

Anyhow, a couple of days later Mom baked one of

her blueberry coffee cakes and took off for T. R.'s. But I don't think she did it just to pay him back. I think she wanted to see who it was I was spending time with.

When she came back, she said, "It felt so odd seeing someone else living there, Lily. But I'm glad it's T. R. He was very friendly, and we had a nice talk. Only he didn't have much to say about himself, and I didn't want to pry. He seemed so alone I asked him to have dinner with us one night. He looked like he could use a good home-cooked meal." If there's anything Mom likes more than keeping everything even between people, it's being one up on them.

❧   *❧*   *❧*

The next afternoon when I was finished at the store, I stopped in to see how the tanager was doing. "That mother of yours is a first-class cook," T. R. said. His mouth was stuffed with blueberry coffee cake.

The tanager had started flopping around in a zippy way. T. R. kept the bird in a box on a table. Spread out on the table were parts for his model airplanes. When I asked what he was working on, he got so quiet and sad-looking I changed the subject. "Do you listen to the river at night?" I asked.

"I'm too busy reading or thinking at night."

"Don't you sleep?"

He sort of barked at me. "I would if I could but I can't."

"You ought to try listening to the river. It always helped me go to sleep."

❧   ❧   ❧

By the end of the week, the tanager was strong enough to fly. T. R. and I took his box outside and put him on the grass. At first he wobbled a little. In a few minutes he was flapping his wings. We held our breath. The tanager skittered across the grass like it was a runway. It lifted a little and fell down, skittered some more, and was up in the air. It landed on a low branch and then hopped up onto a higher one. It rested there for a minute, then flew out of sight.

I turned to T. R., a big grin on my face. I thought he'd feel happy like I did. Instead, there were tears in his eyes.

"What's the matter? The bird can fly again."

"You once asked me what my job was. I used to be a

pilot." He laughed, but it didn't sound like a laugh. "I used to fly." He swung his wheelchair around and sped up the ramp into his house so fast that he nearly ran over me.

FOUR

The hyperactive Chamber of Commerce was planning a Fourth of July sale kicked off by a parade with floats. Our hardware store was supposed to have a float, but Mom was busy. She said she'd leave the float to Laura and me. Laura knew how to do papier-mâché, so I had the idea of making snake heads for a lot of the store's garden hoses. On the floor of the float we put down a square of fake grass from the store. Then we twined the snake hoses all over it. We used our software from the store computer to make banners that read, CRAWL TO STAR HARDWARE. YOU'LL BE SERPENT OF FINDING WHAT YOU WANT. ADDER UP YOUR SAVINGS. WE'LL VIPER AWAY YOUR PROBLEMS. Charlie said, "I think I'll leave town. I wouldn't want people to think I had anything to do with that."

Mom thought it was pretty funny and even squeezed in enough time to help us make costumes. Laura was a snake charmer, and I was a cobra. I hunched down in a basket and then sort of rose up swaying. The float won second prize. The bank got first prize for a float that was all covered with gold spray paint. The people on the float were dressed like money bags and gave out fake dollar bills. Overdone. Right?

I had told T. R. about the float. Lately he seemed a little more cheerful. At least he showed a little interest when I told him what I was seeing on the land, but I still couldn't get him very far out of the house. So I was surprised when he came to watch the parade. Charlie was working the evening shift, so Mom invited T. R. to have dinner with us. There was a bad couple of minutes when he saw the narrow flight of stairs he would have to get up. At first I thought he was just going to roll back to his van and take off. Instead he said, "Lily, you can take my chair up," and he bumped up the stairs, pushing with his arms.

I guess he saw the look on my face as I watched him, because he said in a sort of testy voice, "I'm just *coping,* Lily. It's what we all do one way or another."

But T. R. really enjoyed Mom's dinner. He ate just about everything but the tablecloth. "It's been a long time since I've had a meal like this," he said.

Mom had gone all out, serving trout the way Dad always liked them, broiled with bacon, and making a chocolate angel-food cake for dessert. I think she appreciated T. R.'s appetite as much as he appreciated her food. Usually Mom doesn't have time for cooking. When it's just the two of us, we have a lot of tacos and frozen lasagna.

I cleared the table, Mom washed dishes, and T. R. dried. Something seemed funny, and then I realized it was the first time since Dad died that there had been a man helping out in the house. It made me go quiet, which even T. R. realized was unusual, so he tried to cheer me up. "Lily, since you know the land so well, come and show me around this week. To tell you the truth, I'm getting a little sick of staying indoors all the time. I suppose it's time I learned the difference between poison ivy and poinsettias."

"Well, for starters you won't find either one on the property." I still couldn't say *your* property.

After T. R. left, Mom said, "I'm glad T. R. is starting to get out of that cabin. I think he's lonely. It's hard living alone."

There was something about the way she said it that made me ask, "Do you get lonely?"

"If you mean do I miss your dad, yes, all the time. If you mean lonely like T. R., no. I have you, Lily." She grinned and put her arms around me. "It keeps me occupied just figuring out what you're going to do next." Mom usually turns serious stuff into a joke.

I was feeling kind of closed in, so I wandered onto the tiny porch that sticks out over the back entrance to the hardware store. Beyond the town the pine trees were changing from green to black and disappearing into the night sky. In the distance I could see a ground fog rising from the river. For the thousandth time I wished we were still living in our cabin.

I sat down and drew my legs up and wrapped my arms around my knees to keep warm. Mom came out with Dad's book on astronomy. Together we picked out the constellations. The Pleiades, the seven daughters of Atlas, though you could see only six of them. They were hidden among the stars so that they wouldn't be captured by Orion. Ursa Major and Canis Major, the bear and the dog. Cassiopeia, whose daughter was rescued from a great sea monster. Mom remembered how Dad used to tell me the stories of the stars. I always liked the feeling that some of the things in that huge dark space above me were familiar, things I could put a name to. I thought pilots like T. R. had once been were brave to fly around in something so enormous.

Even though Mom and I stayed up late naming the stars, it was still hard to fall asleep. I missed the sound of the river. When we lived on the river, I liked to sleep with my window open. The river went chattering away, splashing over rocks, singing to me. I hoped T. R. was listening to the same sound so he could sleep.

❧   ❧   ❧

The next day I went up to T. R.'s place, stopping on the way to give Fleabit some dog biscuits. The Bad Hads had left a sign up in front of their house. It said: NO   TRASPASING   THIS   MEANS   YOU TRASPASERS WILL BE SHOT. Apart from correcting the spelling on the sign, I didn't pay any attention to it.

T. R. actually seemed glad to see me, although he greeted me in his usual gruff voice. "It took you long enough to get here. Let's go."

There were two-track roads on the land left over from lumbering days, so the wheelchair wasn't too much of a problem. T. R. had started using a chair without a motor. "How come?" I asked. "Wouldn't your electric wheelchair be easier?"

"Easier, but I like the feeling of moving on my own." When I started to push aside the branches that might be in the wheelchair's way, T. R. snapped, "I can do that myself, Lily."

I got the message, but it was hard knowing what would make T. R. cross. With T. R. you had to change the subject a lot.

"When Mom and I were looking at the stars last night," I said, "the sky looked so huge. When you were flying, didn't you worry about getting lost?"

"The sky was as familiar to me as the river is to you." He didn't like that subject, either. "Now what are you going to show me?" he demanded.

"We'll start with the pond."

"Didn't know I had one."

"You don't know anything about this land. There it is." We rounded a bend, and the two-track led right to the pond. Deer went there to drink or to hunker down in the water if the black flies were bothering them.

A heron rose into the air, its great wings pumping in slow motion. T. R. looked startled. "What's that?"

"Great blue heron. It was hunting frogs and cray-fish."

"Interesting the way it folds its neck in and trails its long legs. Think of the power in those wings." I knew he was thinking of how he used to fly. He was quiet for a minute; then he asked, "What's that pile of sticks in the middle of the pond?"

"A beaver lodge." I picked up some pinecones and aimed for the lodge. In a couple of minutes an angry beaver turned up. They're night animals, and it was cross at having its sleep spoiled. The beaver kept cir-cling the pond, slamming down its tail on the water each time it passed us. The whacks boomed out like thunderclaps. At first T. R. jumped. But when he got used to the noise, he started laughing. It was kind of a stiff laugh, like it hadn't been used much.

"How come you don't know this stuff?" I asked.

"It's the sky I know, not the land."

"Mom said you were a test pilot." I wasn't sure if T. R. wanted to talk about this stuff, but I was curious. "What do test pilots do?"

He hesitated, and then he said, "When a company makes a new plane, they need a pilot to take the prototype up and try it out."

"To see if it can fly?"

"A lot more than that. To see if it can fly after dropping 20,000 feet at a thousand feet per second. To see if it can fly coming out of a stall or a spin or on one engine."

"That sounds dangerous. Weren't you afraid?"

"I knew test pilots who had been in trouble, but I never thought anything would happen to me. I flew all the time. You have to if you want to be a good pilot. I thought the sky was my friend. I thought we understood one another. I guess I thought I owned it. When my plane crashed, I felt the sky had tricked me. I was through with it."

As angry as I was with the river, I couldn't imagine

what life would be like without it. "Won't you ever be able to fly again?"

"What's the point? Who would hire someone like me to test a plane?"

"Why did you move up here and build the fence?"

"Everyone I knew—even my friends—stopped really seeing me. All they saw was this wheelchair. They wanted to do everything for me. I felt as though I was getting smaller and smaller. It was like some crazy magician's trick. I was afraid I'd disappear altogether. I guess I wanted to prove I didn't need anyone.

"One day I got in my van and headed north. When the cities ended and I got into the country, I started looking around for some property. I wanted a place where I could be by myself. But I'm not sure I did the right thing. Just sitting around alone all day doesn't prove very much. I guess I realized that yesterday. I really enjoyed the parade, and by the way, your Mom's a great cook."

I don't know why but I lied. Me, Lily, who can't tell a lie. "Oh, we eat like that all the time. She just loves to cook." I was talking up my mom to T. R. Why?

It wasn't long before T. R. started losing interest in

the stuff I was pointing out. So I stopped playing tour guide and just paddled us back to the cabin. I knew how T. R. felt. It's hard to figure out things that are bothering you when you have to make conversation.

I had left my bike propped outside the gate. When I went to get it, I found two flat tires. I guess I should have been suspicious. One tire could have been a leak, but two tires was strange. I thought I must have ridden over some glass or tacks. I started toward town, still thinking it was things that had done it, not people, when the Bad Hads passed me in their truck. You can always tell their truck. It's plastered with bumper stickers, mean "down with something" stickers.

I was minding my own business when the two Hads stuck their heads out of the truck and grinned at my bike. They slowed down, and I thought they were going to put the bike in the bed of the truck and give me a ride into town. But when I got near the truck, Hadley shouted, "You tell that friend of yours he better take down that fence before deer huntin'! And you keep away from our place." Then they laid a little rubber on the road and took off, leaving me with dust on my face and sand in my hair. So I knew the flat tires were no accident.

Luckily Sheriff Bronson came along. He put the bike in his trunk and drove me into town, so I got to listen to his police radio on the way. But there weren't any robberies in the county or anything else interesting.

FIVE

Every July the Chamber of Commerce organizes canoe races on the Sandy River. It's part of the annual Heritage Day celebration. In the afternoon there's a canoe race for kids, and in the evening a big race for adults that goes all night. My dad had won a whole lot of those races. Now that I was twelve, I was eligible for the kid's race, which only lasts an hour. Mom said she'd give me the time off to practice, but I needed a partner. I thought I had lucked out when Mr. Bennett came into the store for some paint and told me that his son Andy, who was in my class, had fallen rollerblading and broken his arm. Of course I was sorry for Andy, who is not entirely awful and has a great collection of rocks. What it meant, though, was that

Justin Ruffner had lost his partner for the race.

I hiked over to the Pizza Shop, where Justin hangs out. Justin was sitting by himself. I got a Coke from the counter and slid into Justin's booth. Justin's dad raises ostriches. He's got three of them, and each one cost several thousand dollars. Our class got to make a field trip to see them. Mr. Ruffner showed us one of their eggs, which could make an omelet big enough for a dozen people. The thing is, Justin has to take care of the ostriches and he hates them. They're mean and can hit you with their legs. Justin spends a lot of time hiding out at the Pizza Shop. Also, he won't eat eggs.

"What's the matter?" I asked. "You look down."

"Andy fell and broke his arm. That leaves me with no partner for the race." He was shredding the paper slipcover from a straw.

"I heard. I could be your partner."

Justin dropped the bits of paper and looked at me. What his face registered was shock. "You've got to be kidding. Race with some girl. No thanks."

"I'm not 'some girl.' I'm me, and I can handle a canoe as well as you can. I know the river, too. Every inch of it. Better than you know it."

For just a minute I thought he was going to say yes. I held my breath. Then he shrugged. "So what? I'm not turning up at the starting line with a girl."

"You're a pig, Justin."

"Oh, come off it, Lily. Your dad won the race when he was in high school. Can you see him paddling with some girl?"

"Yes, I can. He taught me plenty of tricks paddling. I could probably beat you."

"Go ahead. Anyone can enter. Find yourself a partner, but it won't be me." I guess he saw the disappointment on my face. "Hey, nothing personal. That's just the way it is. Let me buy you another Coke."

"No thanks. I've got to be getting back to the store."

That left Laura. The thing about Laura is that she's really agreeable. She would say yes even to something she didn't want to do. So I had to be honest about everything when I asked her. What I said was this: "For the next two weeks how would you like to get up at six o'clock in the morning and spend the day in the hot sun breaking your back paddling the same stretch of the river over and over?"

"Sure," she said. That's Laura.

"Are you absolutely, positively certain?"

"Sure. Maybe we could paint flowers on the canoe."
I talked her out of that.

Laura really surprises me sometimes. It happened
on our first day of practice. She hadn't done a lot of
canoeing, so I was telling her all this stuff about the
river. We were on a stretch dotted with cedar trees that
grew like small islands in the middle of the river. I was
calling out directions. "Left, keep to your left there,
then a quick right." She was paddling sort of daintily,
as if she were dressed in a long white dress and a big
hat with flowers. Of course she wasn't. She had on cut-
offs and a Chamber of Commerce Rivertown T-shirt.

Behind us we heard the noise of paddles cutting
through water. A canoe with Justin Ruffner and Steve
Blanken rounded a bend and started gaining on us.
Justin had recruited Steve. Steve had gotten into trou-
ble once in fifth grade for starting a rumor on the
Internet that gold had been discovered in the Sandy
River. For a couple days there were license plates in
town from as far away as Minnesota. His family didn't
mind, though. Steve's father is president of the
Chamber of Commerce.

"Hey, Lily," Justin called out. "I see you got another girl to race with you. Why don't you tell her what the paddle's for."

Laura didn't say anything. She just started paddling like we were going in the opposite direction of Niagara Falls with no time to spare. I could hardly match her stroke. Laura is really nice, but she expects other people to be nice, too. If they aren't, watch out. If Laura had only been listening to me when I tried to warn her about which way to go around the island, we would have beaten them instead of ending up stuck on logs lying on the river bottom.

It was Laura who had the idea of talking to Wayne Sloger. Wayne had won the adult race three years running. He works at his dad's gravel pit. Laura knows him because he's married to her aunt's sister-in-law. He was trundling wheelbarrows full of gravel back and forth while he was talking with us. We sort of trotted along behind him. I was trying not to stare at a tattoo on his right biceps. It was a picture of an accordion that kept squeezing open and shut while he worked.

"You got to start the race with heavy paddles," he told us. "Bull your way down the river. When you've gone about a third of the way, you change to light graphite paddles. When you make the change, it's like taking pounds off your shoulders." Laura was writing down what he said in a little notebook. He put the wheelbarrow down and looked at us. "Tell you what. You meet me at the Dogtown landing at six tonight, and I'll give you some pointers."

What with Wayne's pointers and practicing about twelve hours a day and the map Laura made for herself of every inch of the river and something else that was a big secret, we actually thought we had a chance.

The day of the race, Rivertown's streets were crowded with cars. Banners hung from wires strung across the main street. The Heritage Day celebration was underway. A few women were in old-fashioned costumes, their long, full skirts and bonnets sort of weirdlooking in the the middle of the traffic. There was an annual contest for the longest beard, and you could hardly recognize the men behind their scraggly whiskers. Charlie usually won because he had a head start. The supermarket, our hardware store, and May's Country Cupboard all had sidewalk sales. On one of the street corners, Pastor Kuhlman, dressed up like a clown, was making balloon animals for the kids. Students from the high school were driving up and down, hanging out of car windows, shouting to one another. The main event didn't start until nine that night.

Laura and I were the only girls in the kids' race. There were six canoes entered, but Justin and Steve were the ones we had to worry about. The other racers didn't really know the river. They were in it for the fun. At the sound of the starter gun, each team grabbed their canoe and made a dash for the river. I could hear Laura's parents, the Schwans, and Charlie and Mom and my third-grade teacher, Miss Bellfer, who was always talking about our personal best, cheering for us. Mr. Blanken and the whole Chamber of Commerce were cheering for Justin and Steve.

We hit the water with a splash and catapulted ourselves into the canoe. In seconds we were shooting down the river. The day was perfect. The river was gold where the sun was shining. In the shade it was green from the reflection of the trees. People were lined up all along the river to watch the race. As Laura and I passed my old place, we saw T. R. sitting in his wheelchair on the landing. He gave us the thumbs-up sign. Our hours and hours of practicing together had paid off. We left all the other racers behind except for Justin and Steve, who were about two canoe lengths ahead of us.

Laura and I started out by calling out encouraging things to each other, but it took too much breath so we had to stop. The sun was hot, and in spite of a band I had around my forehead, the sweat was running into my eyes. I couldn't stop paddling to wipe it off, so I had to keep blinking to see. Laura was having trouble, too, and she didn't know the river like I did. So we started having some problems. We shot around small islands of tamarack trees growing mysteriously out of the water. We nearly hit a sandbar. Once I had to call out, "Laura! Look out! On your left!" Three sharply pointed stumps stuck up like pickets in a fence. We just missed them, the canoe grazing the edge of the last stump. But we weren't the only ones having trouble. Ahead of us we heard Justin call out to Steve just in time to keep him from being swept out of their canoe by an overhanging branch. The other canoes were well behind us.

About a mile from the finish line, we came to the island in the middle of the river where Laura and I had been grounded our first day. This was one of the river's trickiest places. If you paddled to the left of the island—which almost everyone did—you lost time because it was the longer way. But if you went to the right, you got stuck on logs that lay just below the surface of the water. Wayne Sloger had pointed out to Laura and me that because we weighed less than the boys, our canoe could almost pass over the logs. By the time we got to the island, we had nearly caught up with Justin and Steve. They paddled to the left. We headed for the right side.

When he saw what we were doing, Steve yelled, "We'll come and pry you loose after we win the race!" He and Justin were laughing so much they could hardly paddle. But Laura and I had the last laugh. Our canoe slipped right through the gap without so much as a scrape.

What had happened was this. The night before the race, Laura stayed at my apartment. We waited until midnight so no one would see us, and then we sneaked down the stairs and out the back door. Earlier, after

Charlie had left the store for the day, I had borrowed a small shovel and the trusty crowbar. With the shovel and the crowbar strapped to our bikes, Laura and I headed for the river. It took us twice as long as it would have in the daytime to make it to the place in the river where the island was. Luckily there was a full moon, so we had a kind of silver pathway to follow.

First we had to shovel the sand away from beneath the logs. Because of the current, the sand kept shifting back, so it took a while. When we got enough sand shoveled away, we pried the logs loose with the crowbar and sent them down the river. That left a slot deep enough for our canoe to pass through.

That did it! Laura and I hit the finish line a second before Justin and Steve.

They couldn't believe their eyes. They looked at us as if we were ghosts or something. As if maybe we had been flown there by some spirits instead of actually paddling. Anyhow, Justin was pretty good about losing. He congratulated Laura and me and actually shook our hands, pumping them up and down long enough to be sure the photographer from the *Avalanche* got his picture. I thought of a lot of snotty things to say, but I didn't say them. It's easy to be nice when you win.

As soon as they had seen us paddle by, people had climbed into their cars and headed for the finish line. The Schwans and Mom and Charlie rushed up to congratulate us. Mr. Blanken looked plenty unhappy, but he was polite to us when he awarded the first-place prize: two catcher's mitts. I've got mine in my room because I plan to go out for the girls' baseball team in high school. Laura has hers hanging in her bedroom with dried flowers coming out of the fingers.

In their article about the race, the Rivertown *Avalanche* told how my dad had won the big race three times in a row. The headline read, LIKE FATHER, LIKE DAUGHTER.

When I finally had a chance to be alone on the river, I laid a wreath of field daisies and Queen Anne's lace on the water.

I guess winning the race should have made me forgive the river. Instead, all I could think about was that if it hadn't been for the river, Dad might have been there to see it happen.

SIX

In August the weather turned hot. A week went by with no rain. The bracken in the woods shriveled. There were more birds dipping into the river for water. The squirrels hung out in the shade, sprawled over the tree branches like small rugs. I worried about Fleabit because he was chained outside in the hot sun. I took to checking on him and bringing him water when the Bad Hads were away. The heat was really getting to Fleabit. When I unhooked him from the chain, instead of chasing his tail like he usually did, he just lay there and panted like a steam engine.

Finally I couldn't stand it anymore. Monday morning I called Betty Nestor, the animal rescue officer, and told her about Fleabit. I thought she would make the

Bad Hads keep him out of the heat. Instead, I got myself into a mess.

On Thursday when the Rivertown *Avalanche* came, there it was on page three, along with the names of the people who had been arrested for speeding or burning trash without a permit. The paper said the Durwood brothers had been fined thirty-five dollars for leaving their dog unattended in the hot sun.

Thursday afternoon, the Bad Hads stormed into the store and marched up to Mom. Hadden announced in a voice loud enough for the whole town to hear, "We know who turned us in. That dog's not worth its keep. You can tell that nosey girl of yours we took our dog to the pound. They're puttin' it away. See how she likes that." Then they marched out before I could get my hands on them.

I vaulted onto my bike. The ten minutes it took me to get to the Animal Rescue Shelter were the longest ten minutes of my life. It was just outside of town in one of those little concrete buildings that look like someone started a house and didn't finish it. I burst through the front door. "Is he dead?"

Betty just stared at me.

"Fleabit. Did you kill him yet?"

"Lily, we don't 'kill' animals. We put them away. That's very different."

"Well, they end up dead. What about the Bad Hads' dog?"

"We only put them away when we can't find a home for them or when their owners, for a good reason, ask that we do. If you're talking about the Durwoods' dog, we still have him."

I started breathing again.

Betty shook her head. "I have to admit it doesn't look too good for him. He's not exactly the kind of dog that people are looking for. He's old, half-starved, and covered with fleas."

"How much?"

"How many fleas? Millions."

"No. How much to buy him."

"Well, whoever bought him would have to pay for his shots and a flea dip and his license. Maybe twenty-five dollars."

"I'll take him." I had that much saved from the money I was making in the store. It was the money I was putting aside to buy waders to fish the river.

"Well, that's nice, Lily, but you're underage. You'll need a note from your mother."

"You won't kill him before I get back?"

"Lily! Stop using that word!"

I made her swear on a stack of dog-license applications she wouldn't put him aside or whatever.

Mom was horrified. "Lily, I can't take on any more responsibility. I have the store. I have the housekeeping. I have you. That's more than enough. And it wouldn't be fair to the dog. We live in an apartment."

"If you had a choice between being dead and living in an apartment, which would you pick?"

"I'm not a dog, Lily."

"Just tell me what to do. I'll be your slave. I'll mop the kitchen floor. I'll clean the toilet. I'll straighten my room twice a day." I had an inspiration. "I'll do the ironing." Mom says heaven will be entirely wash-and-wear.

She wrote the note.

Mom brought home a dog bed from the store and a flea collar and a leash. When she got a good look at Fleabit, she was horrified. "That dog looks like a skeleton, Lily." Mom's a great one for feeding people up. She put real hamburger in Fleabit's dog food. He seemed restless in the apartment, so I took him for a couple of walks. That night he did a lot of pacing and finally fell asleep with his nose at the crack under the front door.

The next morning I took him for another walk, filled his water dish, pulled the shades so it would be cool, and promised him we'd be up from the store for lunch. Mom has yogurt with a sliced banana mushed into it, which I can hardly bear to watch her eat. I have peanut butter and onion sandwiches, which she can't watch me eat.

When lunchtime came, Mom and I went up the stairs together. She was the first one in the apartment. When I heard her scream, I thought something had happened to Fleabit. It was the apartment something had happened to. The screens were chewed; the door was chewed; the laundry was scattered everywhere; a vase of flowers had been knocked over, making a puddle on the rug. At least I hoped the puddle came from the vase and not Fleabit. When I saw the look on Mom's face, I knew what was coming.

"It will cost me at least a hundred dollars I don't

have to clean up after that animal. You take him to the animal shelter this minute, young lady."

Mom had only called me "young lady" a couple of times before in my whole life, and each time she meant business. I put Fleabit's leash on him and dragged him off. What I hadn't realized was that Fleabit was an outdoor dog. Even though he had been chained up, he was used to being outside. I guess he thought being tied up outside was better than being shut up in an apartment. I couldn't argue with that. But I didn't want him put away, either.

When I got to the shelter I kept right on going to T. R.'s place. I opened the gate and led Fleabit up to the door. Before I could knock, T. R. had the door open. He took one look at the dog and started to laugh. "That's a sorry excuse for a dog."

"He's a present for you."

"Very thoughtful of you, I'm sure, but no thanks. A sick bird is one thing. A mangy, bedraggled beast is another. Anyhow, he looks like he's your dog."

"He's got to be outside. If you don't take him, he'll be put away."

"Probably the best thing that could happen to him."

Before I could stop myself, I was shouting, "He's not like you. He doesn't care if he isn't perfect. He doesn't want to just give up like you're doing."

T. R.'s face got all red. "So you think this useless dog and I make a perfect couple?"

"That dog's not useless. Not if you love it."

T. R. just stared at me. Even I could see I should have shut up long before. I started to walk away, pulling the dog after me. Fleabit had picked up the smell of a rabbit or a woodchuck and didn't want to come.

"Wait, Lily." I turned around and saw T. R. sitting there, looking at Fleabit like he was some kind of awful-tasting medicine he had to swallow.

"I'll take the mutt," he said. "What's his name?"

"Fleabit."

"Perfect. But you're to give me your solemn word you will bring me no more pathetic creatures: no polar bears with colds, no camels with sore humps, no elephants with unhinged trunks. Also, I will regard this animal as yours, not mine. You will be expected to visit it regularly. What you need, Lily, is someone to fly chase on you."

"What does that mean?"

T. R. gave me one of his crooked smiles. "When a test pilot sets off on a dangerous flight, another pilot flies along right beside him to make sure he doesn't get into trouble."

SEVEN

I dropped in on T. R. and Fleabit every night after supper. One evening I came by canoe. T. R. was sitting in his wheelchair at the edge of the river with Fleabit by his side. Fleabit was gnawing on an enormous bone.

"You're pretty good at handling that canoe," he called out. "You want a passenger?" He tied the dog to a tree, leaving the bone next to him.

I was really pleased but a little nervous about T. R. getting into the canoe. I steadied it against the landing while he maneuvered himself out of the wheelchair and onto the landing and then into the canoe. The strength in his arms made up for his not being able to use his legs.

T. R. sat in the bow of the canoe, his back supported by the seat rest. I sat in the stern so I could steer. He caught on to the paddling fast, and in no time we were skimming along like a team.

"How come you wanted to come canoeing?" I asked.

"Boredom, my child. I don't suppose you know what that word means?"

"You wouldn't say that if you had been in Mr. Macker's social studies class with me. Anyhow, if you're bored, why don't you try flying again?"

"You just don't give up on that subject, do you?" T. R. looked at me, his blue eyes sharp and bright as a bird's, then looked away. "I'd have to go back to the city where there are special planes equipped for paraplegics. That means seeing other people and listening to their stupid questions. Or maybe I just don't want to see them seeing me."

His unhappiness took all the talk out of me, but there was plenty for us to look at. The sand and gravel on the river bottom sort of danced as the current hurried over it. The reflection of the pine and birch trees made stripes of white and green on the water. Dragonflies in bright blues and reds skimmed just above us. They touched down in little swoops on T. R.'s hat and my hands. A kingfisher kept a little ahead of us, teasing us with his rackety laugh as he dove for minnows. A water snake poked up its head, caught a glimpse of us, and disappeared.

"It's getting dark," T. R. said. "Better turn back."

"Just one more bend," I coaxed. "Anyhow, I know the river with my eyes closed. Can you imagine what this river was like back when it was jammed with millions of logs on their way down to the sawmills? Dad said thousands of houses in Detroit and Chicago were built from the logs that floated down this river. They even floated rafts down the river with whole kitchens on them to feed the loggers. We have pictures of them in our family album." T. R. actually seemed interested in what I was saying. It was the first time I had seen T. R. when he wasn't as twitchy as a chickadee around a hawk.

As we rounded a bend, we could make out a deer in the middle of the river, feeding on watercress. We let the canoe drift until the deer caught our scent and raised its head, watercress hanging like a green beard from its mouth. The deer stood looking at us for a long minute, then bounded out of the water and headed for the woods. T. R. turned around and smiled at me. It wasn't one of his twisty, undecided smiles, either. Neither of us said anything. It was the the kind of nice silence I remembered sharing on the river with Dad. I thought back to the evening T. R. had spent with Mom and me and how good it had felt to have him there.

The trout were rising to an early evening hatch of insects. The insects were so tiny they looked like nothing more than a hustle in the air. It was getting darker, and I was about to turn around when I saw a patch of cardinal flowers along the bank. Cardinal flowers don't bloom until late in the summer. These were the first I had seen. I poled the boat over to the shore and picked some. With these and some white ladies' tresses I wove a wreath and laid it on the river.

"What are you doing?" T. R. asked.

"Every Thursday I make a wreath for my Dad. It reminds the river of what it did to him."

"I heard he died on the river, but I don't know why you blame the river."

"You blame the sky . . ." Before I could finish my sentence, I heard something that made me jump. It was the sound of a motor. The river is too narrow and shallow for a motorboat. Besides, the sound of a motor scares away the trout and everything else. The only people who use one are the Bad Hads. They think it's too much work to paddle upriver. And they don't care about the trout. They think the people from downstate who come up flyfishing for trout are wimps. The Hads fish for trout with huge earthworms. Dad always called people who used worms for trout "Plunkers."

Sure enough, the Hads' boat came buzzing along like a rattlesnake. It was headed straight for us.

"What do you fools think you're doing!" T. R. yelled at them. "You must be crazy!"

Probably they just meant to give us a scare, but T. R.'s shouting at them made them see red. They just kept coming. All I could think about was getting out of their way. I started paddling with all the strength I had. The canoe lurched out of their path. They went speeding by, never looking back.

Only I hadn't had time to see where I was steering. Inches ahead of us was a sweeper sticking out from the shore.

"Duck!" I screamed to T. R. in the front of the canoe. It was too late. T. R. got swept into the water. I kicked off my shoes and dove in after him. The water was like ice.

"T. R.!" I called his name. I felt sand under my feet. The next minute the river bottom disappeared and I had to tread water. I was scared that T. R. might have been knocked unconscious by the sweeper. I knew the current would carry him downriver. To find him I would have to let myself go with the river. Water filled my mouth, nearly choking me. I got pitched against a tangle of logs. A second later the river threw me onto shallow bottom where stones scraped my knees. I didn't dare stand up. I had to let the current carry me. It was the only way I could follow T. R. I called his name again and again, but my voice was choked with water.

On a night like this one my father had collapsed, fallen into the river, and drowned. Over and over I had awakened from nightmares of my father struggling in the river. I hadn't been there to help him. Now it was T. R. I had to save him.

The water swept me around a bend, leaving me near shore. I longed to escape from the cold, grabby current. I wanted to climb to the safety of the shore. But I had to let myself be taken up by the river and carried along. Again I called T. R.'s name. This time there was an answer. "Lily? Over here."

The answer came from the near bank. I struggled out of the water. The solid land felt firm and steady under my feet. I could see a dark shape silhouetted against the bank. I was afraid T. R. would be furious with me. Instead, he was laughing! I thought he was out of his head. "Are you all right?"

"Well, all things considered, I guess so. I'm rather wet, and I'm afraid I tore my pants on a log, but outside of that I'm fine."

"You're not mad at me?"

"Why would I be mad at you? It was those numbskulls who caused the accident. To tell you the truth, I'm grateful to them."

"Grateful!" I dropped down beside him, still panting.

"I had to do something for myself, and I did it. I'll tell you a secret, Lily. Ever since the accident I've felt life was pretty miserable, but when I was in the river and nearly drowning I knew the Lord wasn't through with me. I realized how much I wanted to live. Life suddenly seemed sensational. I've always been a good swimmer. I couldn't use my legs, but I could use my arms. So here I am." He smiled at me—a full smile.

I still had a choking feeling in my throat. "I thought . . . I was afraid . . ."

"I know, Lily. But I'm all right." T. R. put an arm around my shoulder. "Now how are we going to get home?"

"I know where we are. It's only a quarter mile to the road. I'll flag down a car."

"What about your canoe?"

"It'll be downriver, snagged along the shore some-place. Everybody on the river knows whose canoe it is."

The first car to come along was Merton Smith's. Merton sells real estate and has a cellular phone glued to his ear most of the time, like there were bunches of houses to sell in Rivertown instead of one or two a year. He called for an emergency medical unit with a wheel-chair. In an hour's time, T. R. was home and so was I.

🌿　　🌿　　🌿

When she saw me squish into the apartment, with my wet hair and clothes, Mom looked like she had seen a ghost. "Lily! What happened? You're soaking wet!" She hung on to me like I was drowning right there in front of her. I knew she was thinking of Dad.

When she heard my story, she exploded. "Those Durwood twins are going to have to answer to me. And Lily, I want you to promise me never to be on that river after dark."

I promised, planning to talk Mom out of it later.

That night I waited for the nightmares to return. Nightmares where I kept dreaming of my father's drowning. But they didn't come back—not that night or any night after that. I guess my saving T. R. took the nightmares away. It was like the eagle I once saw swoop down and snatch a duckling and fly off to make a meal of it. For a long time after that I hated eagles. But they're so majestic and beautiful. Sometimes you see them soaring over the river like kings and queens. After a while I forgot about the duckling and started liking eagles again. Just as I had forgiven the eagle, I had forgiven the river.

EIGHT

Summer was almost over. Laura and I had already gone shopping for new jeans for school. (We got the same kind, only Laura always irons creases in hers and patches them with lace.) On our old property the bracken turned brown and the goldenrod yellow.

Most of the time T. R. stayed cheerful. He started calling friends downstate and getting phone calls back. He even started shopping right in town. Soon everyone recognized his van and his wheelchair. As he wheeled up and down the aisles of the supermarket, people waved or called out to him. He hung out in our hardware store, too. He said he came to buy stuff for his model planes, but I noticed he talked to Mom a lot.

He was in the store the day the Bad Hads came in.

It was the first time any of us had seen them since that night on the river. I was standing next to T. R. I started to shout something angry at the Hads, but T. R. said, "Let me take care of this."

He was in the household aisle, so he grabbed a mop, let out a blood-curdling war cry, and headed full speed for the Bad Hads.

One look at this wild-eyed avenger waving this weird weapon at them, and the Hads were out the door. We all laughed so hard we cried.

Later that week, when I saw a van I hadn't seen before parked next to T. R.'s cabin, I thought a friend from downstate was visiting. As I got closer, I could hear an argument going on. A man in a wheelchair rolled out the open door, past T. R., and got into the van. "Just let me know when you're ready," he called out to T. R. "And stop being so mule stubborn!"

I watched him drive away and then headed up the path to T. R., who was looking plenty upset. "Who was that?" I asked.

"He customizes planes."

"What does that mean?"

"He builds planes that people like me and like him

can fly. I sent him some ideas. He incorporated them into one of his planes, and now he wants me to test it."

"Does that mean you're going to fly again?"

T. R. shook his head. "I'm thinking about it, but I'm not all that anxious for the sky to get hold of me again."

❧ ❧ ❧

By the end of August, T. R. was getting restless. One afternoon when I stopped by in my canoe, he said he wanted to learn to fish. "I've got to get out of this cabin. It's beginning to feel like a coffin."

I had been afraid that after he nearly drowned in the river, he'd never want to get into my canoe again. But he did. "It's like getting back on a horse after you fall off," he said as he settled into the boat. I wanted to say something about getting back into a plane, but for once I shut up.

Some of the maple trees along the bank were beginning to turn. The red-winged blackbirds were strung along the power lines, ready for their trip South. Acorns were plopping off the oak trees.

I tied a hopper fly on the end of T. R.'s line and showed him how a lot of the action of casting was in the wrist. I could tell right away he wouldn't make a real fisherman. He tried to look interested in the fishing, but his heart wasn't in it. When the fly settled on the water, he didn't hold his breath waiting for a trout to rise. He snagged his line in the overhead branches. He pulled his fly up before the trout could take it. When he finally did catch a trout, he just yanked the fish out of the water as if it was no big thing.

He seemed impatient. Like the canoe was too small for him. Finally he said, "I'm not like you, Lily. Land and water aren't enough for me. Everywhere I go I bump into barriers. I can't get my wheelchair through half the doors in this town. I need space in the sky where I can move around. I need to get up there in the sky where I belong. I think I'm going back to the city."

I stopped paddling and looked at T. R. "What do you mean? Like for a visit?"

"Longer than that. I've been doing a lot of thinking lately, and the man you saw a few weeks ago has been keeping after me. The plane is all ready to be tested. I'm going down to take a look at it."

It was like being kicked in the stomach. It had never occurred to me that T. R. would go away. I was just getting used to him. And he was over at our place for dinner all the time. And Mom liked him. "We have an airport near here," I reminded him.

"It's just for small planes. I'd need something with more facilities."

I had trouble getting the question out. "When would you leave?"

"I'm not sure yet, but you'll be the first to know."

And I was. The evening before Labor Day, T. R. came over to see us. We heard him bumping up the stairs. Mom and I were resting up from the Chamber of Commerce's Christmas-in-September sale. The three of us watched a rerun of "Murder, She Wrote" and ate Mom's triple-chocolate-chip cookies, which T. R. said were the best he'd ever had. All of us sitting there together seemed just right. I didn't want T. R. to go away.

When the TV was turned off, T. R. looked at my mom and said, "I made up my mind today to go back to flying. It looks like I'm going to be gone for some time. I wonder if you and Lily would consider renting your old place?"

"Thanks, but we couldn't afford it," Mom said.

There was disappointment in her voice.

"You can have it for whatever you'd get for renting out this apartment to someone, so it wouldn't cost you a penny more."

I couldn't believe it. Mom was shaking her head No. "I appreciate the offer, but the cabin is worth a lot more than anything I'd get for this place. You wouldn't have any trouble renting it to someone else."

"Mom!" I was horrified, but I remembered how she had sold the property in the first place because she didn't want to owe anyone anything.

T. R. tried again. "I don't want to rent it to someone I don't know. The thing is, you'd be doing me a favor by staying at the cabin. If I leave it empty, the Durwood twins will move right in."

Mom wouldn't budge. She only said, "The store's doing better. If you decide to stay downstate, maybe I'll be able to buy the property back at a fair price. In the meantime, we'll be glad to keep an eye on it for you. Lily can check it every day." T. R. could see that Mom meant what she said. After finishing the rest of the cookies, he left.

All that night I kept thinking that T. R. wouldn't be

here to fly chase on me anymore. I had lost my Dad. Now T. R. was leaving. I knew I had to do something. Naturally, when the idea came to me, I didn't think twice. The next morning I didn't even wait for breakfast. I just rushed off to T. R.'s place.

He was packing his model planes. "Morning, Lily. How about giving me a hand with these? If you like you can pick one out for yourself."

"I have a solution to everything," I said. "I know a way to get Mom to move into the cabin. And you won't have to leave."

"You don't understand, Lily. I *want* to leave."

As usual, I wasn't listening. "You can marry my mom. You said she was a great cook and her cookies were the best you ever tasted. And you like each other—I know you do. You could manage the hardware store. Mom hates it, and it would give you something to do. Then we could all live here together."

T. R. just stared at me. After what seemed like an hour he said, "Lily, has your mother indicated an overwhelming desire to be my wife?"

"No, but . . ."

"Lily, I wish I could be a father to you, but I can't.

You had a father, and it isn't me. Even if your mom and I loved each other—and we hardly know one another—I'm not ready to get married. I haven't even figured out my own life and where it's going."

"I'll never see you again," I said. I wanted to smash all the model planes. Planes were taking T. R. away from me.

He must have guessed what I was feeling because he said, "I promise I'll still fly chase on you, Lily. The city is only an hour away by plane."

"What about Fleabit?"

"I talked to Charlie," T. R. said. "He's got a big yard, and I'm throwing in the doghouse with the dog. Fleabit's a hunting dog, and Charlie's a hunter. But Charlie said he'd only take Fleabit if you agreed to keep an eye on him."

I nodded. I couldn't get any words out because I knew if I tried I'd start crying. Fleabit caught a chipmunk just then. It was hanging out of his mouth, wriggling at both ends. I had to get Fleabit to let it go. Fleabit has a soft mouth, and the chipmunk ran off. Luckily I could hide my tears behind my laughing.

Before I left, T. R. and I sat by the river. The tamaracks had turned gold, and a few yellow birch leaves were riding the current. "You ought to take down your fence," I told T. R.

"And let those those sneaky twins tramp around this land? No way."

"It's not just the Bad Hads. Lots of people around here have hunted and fished on the property." I was weaving a wreath of asters and goldenrod to send down the river.

T. R. watched me for a while. "Lily, I'll make a bargain with you. You stop sending those mournful, melancholy wreaths down the river, and I'll take down the fence."

I laid my last wreath on the river. A week later the fence came down.

❧   ❧   ❧

Mom and I went to see T. R. off. We watched his van disappear around the bend of the road. I wondered as I licked them away why tears were salty. And why do you have to keep losing people like the tops off toothpaste tubes or your sunglasses? People ought to come with strings on them to hold on to. But I guess it's like the birds and flowers that come and go. You can't hang on to them. They have their seasons.

I write T. R. to tell him about everything that's happening on the river and how Fleabit's doing. There's snow on the riverbanks now. The ducks and most of the birds have left. The beavers are snug in their lodges, but the otters have made a slide in the snow and take turns slithering down the bank into the river. The river is never covered with ice. In science class we learned that it stays open because of the current. I don't think it's that at all. If something has a heart, it never freezes over.